LETTERS to my DARLING DAUGHTER

Dear Daughter,
This is my love
letter to you...

SUGAR SNAP STUDIO

Quarto.com • WalterFoster.com

© 2024 Quarto Publishing Group USA Inc.
Text and illustrations © 2024 Jessie Ford

First published in 2024 by Walter Foster Publishing, an imprint of The Quarto Group,
100 Cummings Center, Suite 265D, Beverly, MA 01915, USA.
T (978) 282-9590 **F** (978) 283-2742

Walter Foster Publishing titles are also available at discount for retail, wholesale, promotional, and bulk purchase. For details, contact the Special Sales Manager by email at specialsales@quarto.com or by mail at The Quarto Group, Attn: Special Sales Manager, 100 Cummings Center, Suite 265D, Beverly, MA 01915, USA.

27 26 25 24   1 2 3 4 5
ISBN: 978-0-7603-8521-0

Digital edition published in 2024
eISBN: 978-0-7603-8522-7

Diversity and Inclusion Consultant: Yasmin McClinton

Printed in China

To my Darling Daughter,

LIFE IS A JOURNEY!
It has taught me so much.
I want the very best for you—
I want you to know

HOW SPECIAL YOU ARE.

My Darling Daughter

AIR MAIL

Remember, even when I'm not there
to tuck you in at night,
read your favorite story,
or check for monsters under your bed,

I AM STILL
THINKING OF
YOU!

From time to time, I may travel to different places,
BUT I ALWAYS CARRY YOU IN MY HEART.
I love coming home to tell you about my adventures!

I want to INSPIRE AND ENCOURAGE you as you grow up. Here are just a few things I have learned along the way.

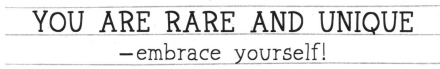

YOU ARE RARE AND UNIQUE

—embrace yourself!

You are one of a kind.
There is only one of you on this planet!
Isn't that cool? Be bold.

BE YOURSELF!

To: My D

CONFRONT YOUR FEARS!
(I believe in you. Yes, I do!)

Sometimes it's exciting to try challenging things that can be scary.

BE BRAVE
—you'll be proud of yourself.

ENJOY THE SMALL THINGS IN LIFE.
There is joy everywhere, if you look for it.

Play is just as important as hard work.
CHERISH THE MOMENTS OF PURE JOY!

BE KIND.

You never know how
someone else might be feeling.
Sad, angry, shy? Perhaps they're
not having a very good day.

ALWAYS treat others
how you'd like to be
treated.

LOVE YOUR BODY—it does incredible things!
Most of the time without us even thinking about it.

Remember that your body is your own.
Cherish it, protect it, and help it grow.

SPEAK UP.
YOU HAVE A VOICE.

Your opinion MATTERS!

It's good to feel strongly
about something and stand up
for what you believe.

Don't worry, accidents happen! Whoops!
It's what we do next that matters most.

GO EASY ON YOURSELF AND TRY AGAIN.
Often, we learn the most when
things don't go as planned.

To: My Darling Daughter

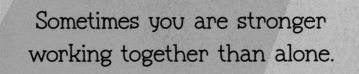

Sometimes you are stronger
working together than alone.

IT'S FUN TO WORK AS A TEAM!
Friendly competition can be exciting.

My Darling Daughter

_____

_____

Success comes in many forms.
So long as you're progressing,
IT DOESN'T NEED
TO BE PERFECT.

Remember, hard work pays
off in the end. JUST KEEP
TRYING YOUR VERY BEST.

63

TREASURE YOUR FRIENDSHIPS!

It feels good to laugh
and be silly with others.
Life is much more fun
with friends to share it.

It's up to us to look after our beautiful planet.
Pick up litter, recycle, plant trees, and enjoy the outdoors!
WHAT OTHER THINGS CAN YOU DO TO
HELP OUR NATURAL WORLD?

And finally, my most important lesson:

LOVE IS THE MOST IMPORTANT THING,
AND I LOVE YOU!

I have loved you from the very first day I met you! You are my most precious bundle of joy.

To my Darling Daughter,

Here is one more lesson—FROM ME, TO YOU: